Countdown To Christmas

A Tree Trimming Service

Lucille Mewhorter

CSS Publishing Company, Inc., Lima, Ohio

COUNTDOWN TO CHRISTMAS

ISBN 0-7880-1044-1   PRINTED IN U.S.A.

*Dedicated to
the children and staff
of the Sunday School
of Peace Lutheran Church,
Lima, Ohio*

Introduction

Countdown to Christmas may be used any time during the Advent season as a children's program, a Sunday School program, or a worship service. For several years our church had found that many of the congregation's children were unable to be in church for the traditional Christmas Eve worship service or the last Sunday before Christmas children's program because of family holiday plans or celebrations. We wanted a program which included as many children as possible and which also incorporated some of the elements of a traditional Christmas pageant.

The program includes an Advent calendar theme, decorating a small Christmas tree, lighting the candles on an Advent wreath, scripture, hymns and carols, reading parts for as many as 25 children (plus four teens, if desired), costume parts for the younger children as the Christmas characters, and one adult part. Most of the parts are read from cards taken off of the Advent calendar, so lengthy rehearsal time is not necessary for most participants.

The children assemble in pews or chairs at the front of the sanctuary. Grandma and Boy/Girl are at left stage near the Christmas tree. The Advent calendar is center stage with the Advent wreath at right stage. As the program progresses, individual children come forward to draw a card out of the Advent calendar, read it to the congregation, and hang the accompanying ornament on the tree. When the Sundays are reached on the calendar, a teen or an older child comes forward to read the Advent wreath message and light a candle on the wreath. At intervals, a hymn is sung by the congregation or children come on stage to sing a carol. Three prophets, Mary and Joseph, shepherds, and angels enter to assemble around the manger at various points in the program.

CAST

The cast includes Grandma, Boy/Girl, three prophets, shepherds, Mary, Joseph, and angels. Readers include four teens or older children for the Advent wreath parts and up to 24 children as readers of the calendar parts. (Some children may read from the calendar more than once if your congregation does not have lots of children.)

PROPS

The props which are needed include a rocking chair, a globe, a small Christmas tree with lights, an Advent wreath with candles, an oversize Advent calendar with pockets, an empty manger, hay, a magic marker, two-dimensional ornaments for each of the days, and typed cards with the readings for each of the days. Some advance preparation is needed to create the calendar, the reading cards, and the decorations.

INSTRUCTIONS

Calendar:

The calendar is made of two red poster boards glued together to form a 28" x 33" card. The dates are made of 4 1/8" x 9 1/2" business size envelopes. Glue the flap down on the inside of each envelope. Cut each to make two square 4 1/8" x 4 1/8" date pockets. Glue the cut edge of each envelope with a narrow line of glue. Use 3-inch numbers and letters to made a December calendar plus any November days that may be needed the year this program is used. Decorate the calendar in a seasonal manner.

Each of the date pockets holds a two-dimensional ornament for the tree and/or a card on which is typed the reading for that day.

Ornaments:

The ornaments should fit the reading, if possible. Make the ornaments as sturdy as necessary and as striking as possible, using glitter, foil, sequins, beads, ribbons, and so forth. Each decoration needs a hanger.

Suggestions for each day:

2nd   — chrismon
3rd   — cross, butterfly, etc.
4th   — child's card with an angel
5th   — flat gift-wrapped package
6th   — manger
7th   — angel
9th   — toy
10th   — bird
11th   — heart
12th   — candy cane
13th   — cookie
14th   — teddy bear
16th   — red bow
17th   — gift card of time
18th   — Trinity symbol
19th   — a stable scene, perhaps cut from a greeting card

7

20th — ornament
21st — musical note
22nd — pot holder
24th — birthday cake
25th — tray favor
26th — question mark
27th — Mary, Joseph and Baby Jesus
28th — candle

Countdown To Christmas

Advent

Scene: *Grandma in a rocking chair, Boy/Girl on a stool at left, with a Christmas tree, untrimmed except for turned off lights, a calendar and an Advent wreath to the right. There is an empty manger at center front stage. There is a globe near Grandma.*

Opening Hymn: "Hosanna Now Through Advent"

Boy/Girl: Grandma, the pastor talked about Advent in church service. What is an Advent?

Grandma: Well, the word "advent" is an old word meaning "coming" or "arriving." Who do you suppose is coming?

Boy/Girl: Jesus?

Grandma: You're right, *(child's name)*. Advent is about Jesus coming to the world and to us. Advent begins on the fourth Sunday before Christmas Day and ends at sunset on Christmas Eve.

Boy/Girl: But what is Advent for?

Grandma: In Advent we remember how the world waited for Jesus' first coming as a baby in Bethlehem and we look forward to his second advent when he will come with power and glory.
Advent began many hundreds of years ago in France. The people wanted to prepare themselves for the Christ

9

Child's coming with extra worship and prayers. In time their good idea spread over all the Christian countries. Customs for this special season have multiplied through the years. You know that people have come from all aver the world to live in our country, don't you? *(Child nods.)* Well, these people brought the Advent customs that we enjoy today. One of them is the Advent wreath.

This began with people in Germany, Sweden, and Norway. *(Grandma points to the countries on the globe.)* These people lived quite far north in the world so when the earth tilted away from the sun during the winter, it was dark there for as many as twenty hours a day. Before they became Christians, those people were sun worshipers, so during the dark winter days they prayed to their hidden sun god to turn the wheels of his wagon and come back to earth. To please the sun god, they took wheels from their own wagons, decorated them with greens and candles and put them in their homes. When these people became Christians, they gave the wreath a Christian meaning. They prayed for the coming of the light which is what Christians sometimes call Jesus: Jesus, the Light of the World.

_____ will tell you how we use our wreath on the First Sunday in Advent.

Day 1 **Older Child or Teen:** Our Advent wreath tells of the dark and waiting world and of the dawning light. Each week the wreath gets brighter as one more candle is lit. On the first Sunday in Advent, we light the first candle on our wreath. Prophet Isaiah wrote, "Arise, shine, for your light has come." Because of this and other prophecies, the first candle is called The Prophets' Candle.

*(Prophets carrying name cards read: **Jeremiah 33:14; Micah 5:2; Isaiah 7:14**. The first candle is lighted.)*

Our circle of light begins. God's plan is to be fulfilled. No one need fear the dark, for the Light of the World shall come.

10

Grandma: Some people use an Advent calendar *(Grandma points to calendar)* to count down the days till Christmas. Others add a decoration to a tree each day *(points to tree)*. Our friends are going to tell you, _____, more about these days of Advent. Would you cross off the date on the calendar each time they tell you about a day? *(Boy/Girl nods and takes the magic marker.)*

(Each "friend" will take a card and a decoration from behind the appropriate date, hold up the decoration, read the card and put the decoration on the tree.)

Day 2 **Child 1:** This is a chrismon, which means a monogram or a symbol of Christ. This is Chi-Rho, the first two letters of Christ in the Greek alphabet. *(Child hangs Chi-Rho on tree.)*

Day 3 **Child 2:** Prophet Isaiah wrote, "There shall come forth a shoot from the stump of Jesse and a branch shall grow out of his roots." Prophecy had said Jesus would be a descendant of King David. Jesse was David's father. Because of these prophecies, some people, during Advent, decorate a branch with religious symbols and call it a Jesse Tree. *(Child hangs a cross or butterfly on tree.)*

Day 4 **Child 3:** Today I'm going to make some Christmas cards. They are going to have angels on them that sing "Peace on Earth, Goodwill to Men." *(Child hangs card decorated with an angel on tree.)*

Hymn: "It Came Upon A Midnight Clear"

Day 5 **Child 4:** Only *(use appropriate number)* shopping days until Christmas. While we're thinking of that, we should also remember that no gift compares to the one God gave us that first Christmas Day. *(Child hangs flat, gift wrapped package on tree.)*

Day 6 **Child 5:** During Advent, some people set an empty manger in their homes. Each time a family member does a kind deed he may put a handful of hay in the manger. Everyone tries to do many good deeds so the baby Jesus will have a soft bed. *(Child hangs manger on tree.)*

(Pre-schoolers and kindergartners put hay in the manger and sing "Away In The Manger.")

Day 7 **Child 6:** In Luke 1:31 the Angel Gabriel said to Mary, "You will bear a son and you shall call his name Jesus." *(Child hangs angel on tree.)*

Day 8 **Older Child or Teen:** On the second Sunday in Advent, God's plan further unfolds. Mary and Joseph leave Nazareth *(they enter from the back and move to one side)* and begin their journey to Bethlehem. So this second candle is called the Bethlehem Candle. *(Light the second candle.)*

Hymn: "O Little Town Of Bethlehem"

Day 9 **Child 7:** December sixth in Holland and Germany is Saint Nicholas Day. Nicholas was a bishop of the church who became a favorite of children because he often carried a bag of gifts for them. Saint Nicholas reminds us of the kind spirit of the Christ Child and of the gifts of the Magi. In our country, Saint Nicholas is often called Santa Claus; in France and England, he is Father Christmas; and in Germany, he is sometimes called Kris Kringle. *(Child hangs toy on tree.)*

Day 10 **Child 8:** My family likes to share the Christmas spirit with the birds who have a harder time finding food when there is a lot of snow. It's fun to watch them gobble up the seeds, suet and bread crusts we put out. *(Child hangs bird on tree.)*

Day 11 **Child 9:** I'm going to help with some extra cleaning at our house today. We won't be ashamed to welcome Jesus, if our homes and hearts are clean. *(Child hangs heart on tree.)*

Day 12 **Child 10:** In Mexico, it is a custom to make a pinata. It is a colorful papier-mache container filled with candy. Blindfolded children try to whack the pinata. The boy or girl who breaks the pinata and lets the candy fall out is the hero of the day. Maybe I'll try to make a pinata. *(Child hangs candy cane on tree.)*

Day 13 **Child 11:** Today my family and I are going to make lots of cookies. We are going to put some of them in pretty boxes and take them to shut-ins who can't make their own. *(Child hangs cookie on tree.)*

Grandma: Some countries have their own special kinds of cookies. Spritz and Pfeffernusse are from Germany; Mandel Skorper from Sweden; Vanilla Krause from Denmark; Columbas from France; Kourabiethes from Greece; Olecakes from England and Gigilena from Italy, to name a few. We'll have some of them to share with everyone in the fellowship hall, won't we, _____?

Day 14 **Child 12:** Christmas is Jesus' birthday. Sometimes we need to think more about what we're giving for Christmas than what we're getting. I've saved some money, so my mom is taking me to the mall so I can buy a gift for a child who might not get any others. *(Child hangs teddy bear on tree.)*

Day 15 **Older Child or Teen:** The third candle is the Angels' Candle. *(Angels enter.)* We who live after Jesus' first coming feel the anticipation of Advent because we can see a promise that has been fulfilled. Just imagine what it must have meant to those who longed for the fulfillment all their lives and did not see it. *(Light third candle.)*

Hymn: "Angels We Have Heard On High"

Day 16 **Child 13:** In Italy December thirteenth is a feast day for Saint Lucia. It is also a special day in Sweden where she is known as Saint Lucy. Lucy was a girl from Sicily who was burned at the stake because she was a Christian. To remember her, the oldest daughter of a Swedish family puts on a white robe with a red sash and slippers and a wreath with candles on her head. Early in the morning, she wakes each member of the family and serves them coffee and special rolls. *(Child hangs red bow on tree.)*

Day 17 **Child 14:** I don't have much money to buy gifts, so I'm going to make some gift certificates of my time for people to "use" after Christmas. *(Child hangs gift card of time on tree.)*

Day 18 **Child 15:** A prayer from the Lutheran Book of Worship is appropriate for this day in Advent: "Almighty God, you called John the Baptist to give witness to the coming of your Son and to prepare his way. Grant to your people the wisdom to see your purpose and the openness to hear your will, that we too may witness to Christ's coming and to prepare his way through your Son, Jesus Christ, our Lord, who lives and reigns with you and the Holy Spirit, one God now and forever. Amen." *(Child hangs Trinity symbol on tree.)*

Day 19 **Child 16:** My Swedish great-grandmother told me about her family's custom of putting straw across one side of a room as a reminder of the stable where Jesus was born. She said the children had fun playing in the straw during the twelve days of Christmas. She didn't tell me who cleaned up all the straw. *(Child hangs stable scene, cut from a greeting card, on the tree.)*

Day 20 **Child 17:** My family and I are going to make decorations for our tree tonight. We're going to string popcorn and make paper chains and lots of different ornaments. *(Child hangs ornament on tree.)*

14

Day 21 **Child 18:** Let's go caroling this evening and sing the good news of Jesus' coming for our neighbors and friends. *(Child hangs musical note on tree. All Sunday School children turn and sing "Joy To The World" to the congregation.)*

Day 22 **Child 19:** Today is Saturday. I'm going to make some Christmas gifts since I don't have to go to school. I have a loom that I am going to use to make pot holders for my grandmother and my teacher. *(Child hangs pot holder on tree.)*

Day 23 **Older Child or Teen:** *(Shepherds arrive.)* The fourth candle is the Shepherds' Candle. The Advent days are almost over. God is faithful; the Son awaits us. Let's reflect the Light of the World in *our* lives as we journey to the manger. *(Light candle.)*

Hymn: "While Shepherds Watched Their Flocks By Night"

Day 24 **Child 20:** It's a custom at my house to make a birthday cake for Jesus. Maybe my mom and I will do that today. *(Child hangs birthday cake on tree.)*

Day 25 **Child 21:** I am going with my class to visit a nursing home. We're going to sing carols for the people there and give them some favors we made for their trays. *(Child hangs tray favor on tree.)*

Day 26 **Child 22:** How many of you have seen the movie *The Sound of Music*? It is the story of the Von Trapp family. Though it is not in the movie, they had an Advent custom they called "It's a Secret." They would draw names on the first day of Advent and then do nice things secretly for that person. They didn't reveal identities until December 23, which is known to some people as the Little Christmas. *(Child hangs question mark on tree.)*

Day 27 **Child 23:** This is that Little Christmas Day. It's a good day to put out the family's creche or nativity scene. *(Mary, Joseph, angels, and the shepherds gather around the manger.)* The tradition of setting up a miniature nativity scene seems to have begun in Italy early in the thirteenth century. Saint Francis of Assisi is given credit for arranging the first creche. *(Child hangs Mary, Joseph, and Baby Jesus on tree.)*

Hymn: "To A Virgin Meek And Mild"

Day 28 **Child 24:** Many customs are associated with Christmas Eve. In France, children have put their oat-filled shoes outside the door for the camels of the wisemen they believed were traveling that night. The Irish put tall candles in the windows to light the Christ Child on his way. Many people use luminaries for the same reason. We have used them here at our church. A legend in many countries is that cattle kneel in their stalls at midnight to honor the birthday of God's Son. Can we do less? *(Child hangs candle on tree.)*

(Light the tree. All the Sunday School children gather behind the nativity scene. Everyone sings "O Come, All Ye Faithful.")

Grandma: We hope we have helped you prepare for a meaningful Advent and a happy, blessed Christmas.

* Readings may be omitted to achieve the appropriate number of Advent days for the year this program is being used. The days of Advent vary according to the day of the week on which Christmas Day falls.

www.ingramcontent.com/pod-product-compliance
Lightning Source LLC
Chambersburg PA
CBHW071814020426
42331CB00009B/2492